Me and my Hair

WRITTEN BY
Kimberley Kinloch

ILLUSTRATED BY
**Jessica Gibson &
Sandra Becker Borrée**

EDITED BY
Katie Daynes

DESIGNED BY
**Eleanor Stevenson,
Tilly Kitching
& Caroline Ryder**

Sometimes my friend Ahmed calls my hair **fuzzy** and tries to pet it, which **annoys** me.

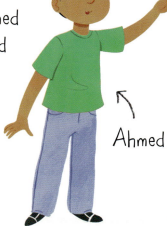

← Ahmed

It's not fuzzy, it's **coily**...

...and I'm **not** a pet.

Mom says I should be PROUD of my hair.

There are **so many** hairstyles you can do with it!

Mom, with one of her many **amazing** styles

 For a special treat, Mom says I can go to her hairdresser. **YAY**.

She warns me that it will take a loooooong time, so I'm going to take a book with me!

But first my friend Mia comes over and we decide to do each other's hair.

HIGH PONYTAIL FOR MIA

Mia's hair is flowy like a river. My brush **glides** through it.

I wonder what it feels like to have flowy hair.

I loop a scrunchie around Mia's hair and make it look like a tail on a pony...

...or a **UNICORN**.

But her hair keeps slipping out. Now I get why she needs so many barrettes!

AFRO PUFFS FOR ME

Next it's Mia's turn to be the hairdresser. I pass her my **detangling moisturizer**.

She squirts some into her hand and rubs it through my hair, so it's easier to comb.

Mia loves how soft my hair is.

Then Mia parts my hair and stretches little bands over each side to make two big **puffs**.

I ask Mia to **lay my edges**, but she doesn't know what I mean. So I get some hair gel and a toothbrush (not the one for my teeth!) and show her.

You gel the wispy baby hair, then brush it down and make a flat, **wavy pattern**.

Afro puffs

Mia is IMPRESSED.

I can't wait to go to the **REAL** hairdresser's.

AT THE HAIRDRESSER'S

I'm sitting on a nice sofa waiting for my turn, and there's **so much** to take in...

THE NOISES
- Buzzy clippers
- People chatting
- Music playing

THE SMELLS
- Fruity shampoos
- Coconutty conditioners
- Smelly creams

Everyone is Black or mixed-race and **lots** of people have Afro hair – **LIKE ME**. Mom says we come here because Afro hair needs its own special care.

EXTENSIONS

There are rows of extra bunches of hair called **extensions**. People have them added to their own hair to make it longer.

Natural shades to match your hair

My cousin Meesh has red ones like this for fun.

Extensions are wrapped around sections of real hair, then braided together.

RELAXING

Afro hair can be straightened using a cream called a **relaxer**.

BEFORE → AFTER

CLIPPERS

Hair **clippers** have different settings for different cutting lengths. You can mix them up to make patterns.

No. 3 for a slightly longer cut

No. 1 for a very close shave

DREADLOCKS

Dreadlocks are locks of hair that twist around themselves as they grow.

I spot my Uncle Joe. He's having his dreadlocks retwisted.

Hi Kyra! Meet Oti. She's a **loctitian** – a dreadlock specialist.

I'm **rolling** the dreadlocks between my palms to keep them neat and tidy.

← Oti

Finally, Mom's hairdresser comes over and it's **MY TURN**.

Mom's hairdresser is **AWESOME**. Her name is Dee, and she knows **so much** about hair.

This is Dee.

She shows me a chart of the different **hair types**.

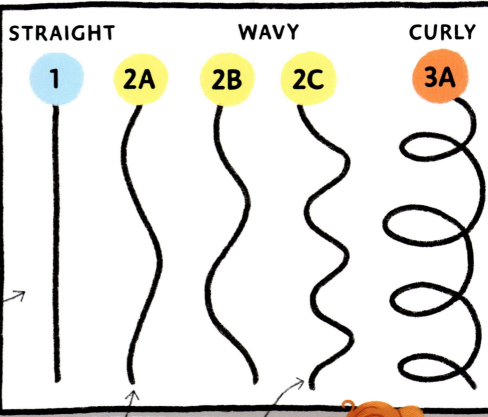

STRAIGHT	WAVY			CURLY
1	2A	2B	2C	3A

My friend Tilly is definitely **type 1**.

I bet our friend Ahmed is **2A** or **2B**.

Mia is more the **2C** type.

My cousin Alex is probably **3B** or **3C**.

Dee says Afro hair is type **4**. It can be **coily** (curling up in tight springs) or **kinky** (made up of tiny zigzags). She says my hair is **4A**.

COILY AND KINKY

3B **3C** **4A** **4B** **4C**

Mom says my brother Tyrone has **4C** hair. But it's hard to tell — he keeps having it shaved off.

Dee explains how hair grows out of little pockets in your skin called **follicles**.

Follicle

My hair!

FOLLICLE FACT

It's the **shape** of your follicles that shapes how your hair grows.

Straight   Curly   Coily

Dee sits me in front of a mirror and asks what hairstyle I'd like. It's a tricky choice!

> I love my coils but keeping them **happy** and **bouncy** takes a lot of time.

I ask what would look good and be easy to look after...

> How about **braids**? They're your hair's best friend. They **protect** it and keep it strong so it can grow.

> Yes please!

First, Dee washes my hair and combs out any tangles.

Next, she blow-dries it to stretch out my coils.

> It's funny seeing myself with straighter hair!

Then she starts braiding my hair in small rows along my head.

She keeps adding moisturizer. It's cold and tickly.

BRAID FACT

These braids are called **cornrows**. They look like neat rows of corn in a field.

HOW TO BRAID

Braids are also known as **plaits**.

I'm getting better at braiding. You take **three strands** and cross them over each other in turn.

For **cornrow** braids you have to collect **extra** hair as you go, adding it to each strand.

Extra hair

Braiding cornrows can take a long time, but you can make all kinds of fun patterns...

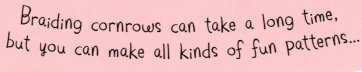

...and you can leave them in for 3 or 4 weeks!

Our soccer coach uses a similar technique to do a **French braid** in her hair.

Mia's mom uses two strands to give Mia a **fishtail braid**.

And Tilly's sister sleeps with her hair in braids, then takes them out in the morning to make wiggly **mermaid** hair!

11

At first, Dee pulling my hair **this way** and **that way** is a bit uncomfortable.

But then Mom hands me some new **soccer stickers** and soon I don't notice what Dee's doing.

I'm too busy creating

MY DREAM TEAM...

...and checking out the players' **HAIRSTYLES**. There are so many different looks.

DEFENDERS

Pompadour with fade

Afro Puffs

GOALKEEPER

My favorite goalkeeper has an undercut. I wonder what that would look like on Tilly.

Curtains

I like the braided bun style. My cousin sometimes has her hair like this.

MIDFIELDERS   FORWARDS

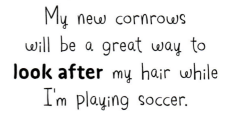
My new cornrows will be a great way to **look after** my hair while I'm playing soccer.

Short dreadlocks

Cornrows like mine!

Top knot

Relaxed bob

I glance up to see how Dee is doing, but she's already finished!

Short back and sides

It's **amazing**. Thanks, Dee!

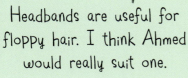
Headbands are useful for floppy hair. I think Ahmed would really suit one.

I'm so **excited** to show my friends my **NEW HAIRSTYLE**. Luckily I don't have to wait long, because Ahmed has invited us to his **tree house**.

Woah! Where did your big hair go?

HA HA! It's all still there, just braided into **cornrows**.

Awesome!

Then Tilly arrives, and she really has had her hair **cut off**. It totally suits her.

It feels great, but today I have sticky-up **BED HAIR**.

zzzz

I tell Tilly she should sleep in a **hair bonnet**. That's what I do. But my friends have never heard of a hair bonnet!

I explain it's a loose, silky cap that stops your hair getting messed up at night. Now they **all** want one!

I like chatting to my friends about hair. It gives us a chance to **understand** each other better.

Me and my **super-long** braids

MIA'S PAGE

Hi, it's Mia here.
Kyra asked me to write about
my hair, so here it goes…

My hair is long, wavy and red. Well, it's really more **orange** than red. In fact, people often call it **ginger**, which is fine by me.

FUN FACT

For thousands of years there wasn't a word for the color orange! People called hair like mine **red**, and the name has stuck.

My **bright** hair makes me stand out in a crowd.

Did you know, less than **2%** of people in the world have red hair.

I **wash** my hair every other day.

It only takes five minutes with my all-in-one shampoo & conditioner.

Every few months I get a **trim**. My hairdresser says snipping off the split ends keeps it healthy.

Healthy end

Split end

I told my hairdresser that I was being **teased** about my hair.

She was shocked and said people **pay** to dye their hair the same color as mine.

That really cheered me up and made me feel pretty **LUCKY**.

I love my hair. It's a **big** part of who I am.
Together, we **BRIGHTEN UP** the room.
OK, I've reached the end of the page now.
Stay awesome.
Love, Mia x

Wow, Mia's hair routine is so different from mine!

It can take the **whole** afternoon to wash, condition and moisturize my hair, but luckily I only need to do this **every other week**.

Saturdays are my **HAIR** day.

Mia says she likes it when her hair gets **wet**, because it goes nice and **wavy**.

But I try to keep my hair **dry**, because Afro hair goes super coily as soon as it's wet and it looks as if it's **shrunk**!

Dry hair

Wet hair

I tell Mia about the big cap I wear to **protect** my hair when I'm swimming.

I even wear it in the **sea**!

Me and my family on vacation in Barbados

Dad and Tyrone have short hair, so they don't wear caps.

Mia asks **why** Afro hair needs extra care, so I tell her what I learned from Dee...

♥ AFRO HAIR CARE ♥

We like to keep our Afro hair **dry**, but we don't want it **too dry** or it might **break**.

Our hair follicles make **natural oils** that help **moisturize** and **protect** each hair... but they don't spread very far along coily hair.

That's why our hair needs **lots** of moisturizer.

Annoyingly, salty sea water and the chemicals in swimming pools can **strip** the oils and moisture from hair. But a swim cap keeps the water out.

DID YOU KNOW?

Until 2022, it was **against the rules** for Olympic swimmers to wear big swim caps. Only small, tight ones were allowed.

Squeezing Afro hair into a super-tight cap is really ouchy and pinchy!

PINCH! PINCH! OUCH!

But now people understand that bigger hair needs bigger swim caps! Then the competiton is **fairer** for everyone.

That evening I ask Dad why my hair is **black** and Mia's is **red**. And why do other people have blond, brown or gray hair?

Dad doesn't know, so we watch a video to find out. It's quite complicated, but this is basically what it said...

SKIN COLOR AND HAIR COLOR COME FROM STUFF CALLED MELANIN.

Hair **melanin** is made in the same follicle pockets as our hairs and natural oils. It can be brown, black or red.

Lots of **black** melanin gives you **black hair**.

Black and **brown** melanin give you **brown hair**.

Just a little **brown** gives you **blond hair**.

Only people with **red** melanin as well have **red hair**!

As people get older, their follicles make **less** melanin, so their hair might go gray or white. Their follicles can change shape too, so their **hair type** might change.

Grandma's hair is less coily than it used to be.

Sometimes follicles stop working and people lose their hair.

← Dad's friend Paul is completely bald.

THE LIFE OF A HAIR

The video told us another cool thing. It's not the **same** hair that keeps on growing from each follicle. Hairs have their own **mini lives**.

A hair grows roughly half an inch each month for around 3 to 7 years.

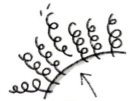

Then it stops growing, falls out...

...and a new one starts to grow.

Luckily the hairs don't all fall out at the same time! They each have different life cycles.

It's hard to tell how long **my** hair is – unless I **S T R E T C H** out the coils.

At school, we're studying leaders from history. Some French kings had **really long**, **curly hair**.

They look very proud of themselves.

My hair is **longer** than yours.

Ah! But mine is much **curlier** than yours!

Our teacher, Mrs. Ademola, says they often wore **fancy wigs**.

Ahmed starts giggling and says he can't imagine kings having long hair or wigs today!

HE HE!

But Tilly says why shouldn't they?

Anyone can have long or short hair. It's up to them!

And we realize Tilly's right. **Lots** of people have long hair.

← Sports stars

← Uncle Joe

My brother's friend Tandeep has long hair under his **patka**.

It's a Sikh tradition.

It gets me thinking about other hairstyles and choices...

HAIR CHOICES

UNFAIR FACT

At my cousins' school, **Black students** weren't allowed to wear **Black hairstyles**. The teachers said they were **messy**.

Big Afros were **banned**...

...and so were cornrows!

None of the teachers making the rules had Afro hair, so they didn't understand what was **best** for it.

Your hair should look **neat** like mine.

But our hair doesn't grow like that!

My cousins were really brave and **spoke out** about why the rules were unfair.

OUR HAIR HAS RIGHTS

YOUR RULES AREN'T FAIR

Luckily the rules have changed now, and more people can **choose** how they wear their hair. **Whew.**

It's only **one more day** until my BIRTHDAY!

Here are the invitations I sent to my friends.

HIP HIP HOORAY! KYRA'S HAIR-THEMED BIRTHDAY PARTY

To ....Tilly....
When ....This Saturday!....
Where ....18 Maple Road....
RSVP (YES) / NO

I've asked everyone to wear **awesome hairstyles**.

Mom lets me choose what goes in the **party bags**.

- Scrunchie
- Bouncy ball
- Barrette
- Pencil
- Comb
- Notebook
- Headband

On the **big day**, Mom ties my cornrows into a little bun, then lays my edges again because they're getting a bit **wispy**.

I can't believe it's finally PARTY TIME.

My friends will be here any second. I am super, **SUPER** excited!

THE PARTY HAIRSTYLES

Me!

Tilly has put **hair chalk** on her hair. It looks like a **rainbow**.

Mia has a **fishtail braid**.

Ahmed is **so** funny. Look at his wig!

Some of the parents have **fancy hairstyles**, too.

Pompadour

Space buns

Pom-pom ponytail

Ahmed's mom is wearing a **beautiful**, flowery scarf. I ask her about it.

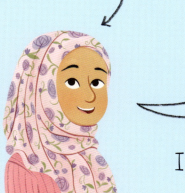

It's called a **hijab**. I cover my hair as a sign of respect to God.

I **love** learning new things like this.

Today was officially the **BEST BIRTHDAY EVER**.

Back in school, we tell our teacher about my party and the amazing hairstyles.

Since today's lesson is on **Black history**, Mrs. Ademola decides to tell us about **Black hairstyles**.

She says Black people have worn braids like mine for **thousands of years**. But the names we call them today – **cornrows** or **canerows** – date back to the time of the **slave trade**.

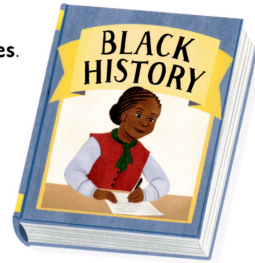

We ask her what she means by the **SLAVE TRADE**...

...and what she tells us next makes the whole class go very, very **STILL**.

Many years ago, African people were **kidnapped** and taken away in ships. They were **sold** to white "masters" and **forced** to work for no money. This was known as the **transatlantic slave trade**.

I own you now. You must grow sugar cane for me!

This is so hard.

How can anyone **OWN** a person?

That's **AWFUL**!

Some Africans braided their hair as an easy way to look after it...

...and the braids looked like the rows of crops they were forced to grow.

Cornrows or canerows became new names for these braids.

People began using their braids to pass on **secret messages** and plan **escapes**.

Five rows means meet at **5pm**.

They even **hid rice** in their braids to eat on their journey!

But **runaways** were **arrested** and **punished** for breaking the law.

SHOCKING FACT

Slavery was **ALLOWED BY THE LAW!**

STOP SLAVERY

Eventually, enough people **protested**...

...and the slave trade was **ABOLISHED**.

FREEDOM FOR ALL!

Abolished means it was made **ILLEGAL**.

I can't believe it was ever allowed in the first place.

When Mrs. Ademola finishes speaking, I run my fingers through my own cornrows. It suddenly feels hard to look at anyone.

It upsets me too, Kyra. But it's only a **part** of our story. You're writing your own story every day.

I look up again, smile and let go of my cornrows.

Later on, I think some more about the things Mrs. Ademola said. I feel differently about my hair now.

I used to just love how it **looks**, but now I love how it makes me **feel**.

I'm **PROUD** of my cornrows...

...and the bigger **story** they're a part of.

I ask my friends and family how they feel about **their** hair.

...or just let it **do its own thing**...

...your hair is a part of **you** and that's really **special**.

Wavy and relaxed

A looser Afro

But it will always be **MY hair**.
And I'll always be **ME**.

This book was written in consultation with
THE HALO COLLECTIVE – an organization of young people fighting to end hair discrimination, while protecting and celebrating Black hair and hairstyles. Here are some of their thoughts, in their own words...

"My hair gives me the **confidence** to be who I want to be." — Kaisha

"I **love** my curls. They remind me to embrace my natural self." — Stephanie

"We're on a **mission** to help everyone learn to love their hair." — Katiann

"My hair is as **unique** as I am, and encourages me to be creative." — Olamide

USBORNE QUICKLINKS
Scan the QR code on the back cover for links to websites celebrating all types of hair, or go to **usborne.com/Quicklinks** and type in the title of this book.

SERIES DESIGNER
Nickey Butler

SERIES EDITOR
Jane Chisholm

DIVERSITY CONSULTANTS
Show Racism the Red Card

HAIR PRACTITIONER & EXPERT
Paris Reveira

First published in 2024. Copyright © 2024 Usborne Publishing Limited. The name Usborne and the Balloon logo are registered trade marks of Usborne Publishing Limited. All rights reserved. No part of this publication may be reproduced, stored in a retrieval system or transmitted in any form or by any means without prior permission of the publisher. First published in America 2024. AE

Children should be supervised online. Usborne Publishing is not responsible and does not accept liability for the availability or content of any website other than its own, or for any exposure to harmful, offensive or inaccurate material which may appear on the web.